# TRIGGERED TO *Heal* WORKBOOK

---

## 16 SACRED PRACTICES TO HEAL DEEPLY

---

### AMANDA D. LIGON, LMSW

# CONTENT ADVISORY

This workbook contains references to childhood sexual abuse, domestic violence, sexual assault, and trauma. While the focus is on healing and empowerment, some content may be triggering for survivors.

As you work through these sacred practices, I invite you to take what serves you and gently release what does not. You are free to move at your own pace, skip practices that don't resonate, and return when ready. This is your journey, and you are worthy of healing, restoration, and peace.

Please proceed with care and compassion for yourself. If you find yourself overwhelmed, it is okay to pause, skip sections, or seek support from a trusted therapist or counselor.

## Crisis Resources:

- National Domestic Violence Hotline: 1-800-799-7233 (SAFE)
- National Sexual Assault Hotline (RAINN): 1-800-656-HOPE (4673)
- 988 Suicide and Crisis Lifeline: Call or text 988

You are not alone. Healing is possible. And you deserve support.

# DEDICATION

This workbook is dedicated to every survivor who was told to stay quiet.
To those who were never rescued.

From the heart of *No Violence No Victim Inc.*, this book is a living testament that you are not broken, you are not alone, and you are never too far from healing.

May every page return you to your power.

*Stillness is not stuckness. It is the space where healing prepares you for movement.*

**— Amanda D. Ligon, LMSW**

———— ♥ ♥ ♥ ————

# PROLOGUE

## *No One Was Coming. So, I Came for Myself.*

During my first marriage, I felt completely stuck. I didn't know what to do or who to do it for first. Should I focus on my younger children? Should I tend to my oldest son, who has carried trauma since childhood? Should I check in with my oldest daughter, who seemed unfazed, though her silence spoke volumes? Or do I finally listen to the part of me that was silenced the night we were married.

I was trying to fix things.
Trying to fix my family.
Trying to fix me.

But nothing was working. And deep down, I was waiting for someone... anyone to tell me what to do.

For years, I sought the opinions of others about my marriage. I wanted someone to say, "Leave him." I wanted someone to tell me that marriage wasn't supposed to hurt like this. I wanted someone to call the police. To intervene. To rescue me. But no one did.

And then one day, I realized no one was coming to rescue me. That was my job. I remember thinking, "This doesn't feel good." That one sentence, that one truth became my lifeline.

That was the moment I filed for divorce. Not because someone told me to. But because I couldn't take one more slap.

One more shove.
One more threat.
One more name that didn't belong to me.

One more night of mind games.

One more lecture blaming me for being raped as a little girl.

One more day of being told I was "F'ed up" from my childhood.

And most of all, I couldn't let another one of my children scream out: "Get off my mommy."

That was the moment I began rescuing myself. But I didn't do it alone. When no one came to rescue me, I learned that God was already there. In the breath I took when I thought I couldn't breathe. In the stillness when I finally stopped running. In the whisper that said, "You are seen. You are known. You are loved. And I am here."

From that point forward, I started listening to my breath, to my body, to the parts of me that had gone quiet just to survive. I began sitting in silence. I practiced grounding myself. I meditated. I took deep and long breaths. I prayed. Not to be spiritual or deep, but to survive and to remember I was never alone.

I stopped trying to earn love. And started learning how to give love to myself. And I learned to receive the love God had been offering me all along.

This workbook was born from that journey. It's not just about rescuing yourself. It's about becoming unstuck. It's about remembering your power. And returning to your body, your breath, your wholeness. It's about discovering that you were never alone, that God has been with you all along, and that healing is both deeply personal and profoundly sacred.

The sacred practices I'll share through breath, faith, movement, prayer, stillness, and self-honesty aren't meant to impress you.

They're meant to walk beside you. They're what I used when I was climbing out of the emotional quicksand of my life.

You might be there now.

Maybe you're stuck because of a toxic relationship, like I was. Maybe it's grief, the kind that lingers and pulls on your joy. Maybe it's the loss of a job, a dream, or a version of yourself you no longer recognize. Maybe it was a breakup that shattered your confidence. Or a season of life where nothing makes sense. Maybe you've just been strong for so long... you forgot how to rest.

Being and feeling stuck doesn't always look the same. But the way out almost always begins the same way: by returning to you. And by remembering that you are not alone. That God is always present.

And if you're in that place right now, let me say this:

- You are not broken.
- You do not have to stay there.
- You don't need anyone else to rescue you.
- You have the strength to reach for your own hand.
- And God is reaching for you, too.

This workbook is your reminder and your invitation to begin again.

Begin again:

- With breath.
- With faith.
- With honesty.
- With you.
- With God.

# TABLE OF CONTENTS

# NOTE TO READER

This workbook is a companion to my memoir, Triggered to Heal: An Invitation to Feel Fully and Heal Deeply, and is designed to guide you through the 16 sacred practices that supported my healing journey. As a licensed social worker, I bring both professional training and lived experience to these pages. However, I share these practices not as prescriptions, but as invitations. What brought me strength and restoration may resonate with you, or it may not. Each healing journey is unique.

This workbook is not a substitute for professional therapy, medical care, or crisis intervention. While I am a licensed social worker, this workbook is a guide for personal reflection and practice, not a therapeutic relationship. If you are navigating trauma, abuse, or overwhelming emotions, I encourage you to seek guidance from licensed therapists or counselors, and trusted support systems. Your safety and well-being matter.

May these practices meet you where you are and walk with you toward healing deeply.

With love and solidarity,

Amanda

# WORKBOOK & MEMOIR CROSS-REFERENCE

| Workbook Practices | Memoir Chapter(s) |
| --- | --- |
| 1 – Breath | Chapter 1, 2 |
| 2 – Faith | Chapter 3, 11 |
| 3 – Prayer | Chapter 9, 11 |
| 4 – Meditation | Chapter 4, 6 |
| 5 – Walking | Chapter 9, 10 |
| 6 – Writing | Chapter 8, 11 |
| 7 – Creating | Chapter 10, 12 |
| 8 – Singing | Chapter 2, 9 |
| 9 – Cold Water | Chapter 5, 7 |
| 10 – Connection | Chapter 9, 12 |
| 11 – Healthcare | Chapter 11 |
| 12 – Therapy | Chapter 9, 11 |
| 13 – Growth | Chapter 10, 11 |
| 14 – Gratitude | Chapter 12, Epilogue |
| 15 – Presence | Chapter 2, 11 |
| 16 – Rest | Chapter 9, 11 |

# INTRODUCTION

Have you ever felt like you were drowning in your own life?

Like no matter how hard you try to breathe, pray, push, or hold it all together, you were still sinking?

I know that feeling. I lived in it for years.

This workbook is a tender, soul-deep invitation into sacred practices that helped me rebuild my life from the inside out. Born from the ashes of abuse, heartbreak, and survival, these sacred practices of breathing, grounding, praying, creating, singing, resting, and more are not about perfection.

- They are about presence.
- They are not about fixing you.
- They are about finding you.

Inside these pages, you'll discover 16 sacred practices that carried me from survival to wholeness. But before I could test any of these sacred practices, I had to believe there was a God who saw me. Before I could pray, I had to trust there was Someone listening to me. Before I could heal, I had to anchor myself in the truth that I was not alone. That the Creator of the universe knew my name, held my pain, and was walking with me through every dark valley.

My belief in God did not erase my trauma; it gave me a place to stand while I faced it. Scripture became my anchor when I felt adrift. Connecting with other believers became my community when I felt isolated. And prayer became my lifeline when I felt like giving up. That's why you will see every chapter in this workbook begins with Scripture. Not to preach, but because the foundation of my healing was (and is) Jesus Christ.

If you come from a different faith tradition or no faith tradition at all, I honor that. The sacred practices I share; breath, movement, creativity, connection... belong to all of us. I invite you to adapt them in ways that resonate with your own beliefs.

Research shows that belief in a Higher Power is a powerful resource for trauma survivors. Studies have found that:

- Positive religious/spiritual coping (seeking spiritual support, trusting in God's love, collaborating with a Higher Power) is associated with posttraumatic growth—the ability to find meaning, purpose, and strength after trauma (Park et al., 2017; VA National Center for PTSD).
- Spirituality provides a sense of not being alone. For many trauma survivors, believing in a Higher Power means they don't have to carry their pain in isolation. This sense of divine presence and guidance has been linked to greater resilience and hope (Larsen & Harris, 2024).
- Faith communities offer social support, which is one of the strongest predictors of recovery from trauma (Harris et al., 2011).
- Spiritual practices like prayer, meditation, and Scripture reading help regulate the nervous system and provide comfort during distress (VA National Center for PTSD).

I am not sharing these practices to persuade you to believe what I believe and certainly not to condemn you if your beliefs differ from mine. My intention is to inspire you to recognize that acknowledging a Higher Power (however you understand that power to be) gives you strength.

It reminds you that you are not alone.

It assures you that you are seen, known, and guided.

It anchors you when everything else feels uncertain.

You don't have to have all the answers. You don't have to have perfect faith. You just have to be willing to take the next breath. Be open to consider that there is a Higher Power who sees you, knows you, and is walking with you toward your healing through these sacred practices.

This isn't just a workbook. It's a spiritual pause. A holy exhale. A soft nudge toward your own hand when triggered. If you've ever whispered, "I don't know how to keep going," let these pages remind you: You don't need to be rescued. You need to remember your power. When life feels too heavy, don't give up, don't give in, and don't throw in your towel. You are being reshaped.

In these pages you will discover:

- Scriptures to anchor you in truth.
- Personal stories that meet you in your pain.
- Grounding practices to help you reconnect with your body and spirit.
- Reflection Prompts that begin with honesty and end in hope.
- Gentle reminders that your healing doesn't have to be loud to be powerful.

*Healing is already happening, one sacred breath at a time.*

# PART ONE

# FOUNDATIONAL PRACTICES

*Returning to the sacred ground of your own being.*
**—Amanda D. Ligon**

# PRACTICE 1
# THE PRACTICE OF BREATH

*"Then the Lord God formed man from the dust of the ground and breathed into his nostrils the breath of life, and the man became a living being."*
**– Genesis 2:7 (NIV)**

This scripture offers one of the most intimate images in the Bible—God breathing into humanity.

He didn't just speak life, He breathed it.

Face to face. Spirit to spirit. Breath to breath.

That divine breath wasn't ordinary air, it was ruach, the Hebrew word meaning both breath and spirit. From our very beginning, we were created to carry the very breath of God within us.

Biologically, breath regulates the nervous system, calms the mind, and signals safety to the brain.

Spiritually, breath anchors us in the present. It reminds us that we are alive, held, and still connected to the One who formed us.

Breath is our first gift. Every inhale quietly declares "I am still here and God is still with me."

# Story Time

In my memoir *Triggered to Heal*, I share the moment I was triggered in a car and my body responded with rage, trembling, and panic (Chapter 1). That experience taught me the power of returning to my breath—the first sacred practice I learned to use when my nervous system was overwhelmed.

After being in birthing rooms many times, I've noticed a gentle, repeated instruction from nurses and doctors alike:

"Breathe."

And not just once, but over, and over again.

Because in the midst of pain, pressure, and chaos, breath grounds us. It reminds the birthing mother that, even in what feels out of control, she still holds something sacred: her presence.

There is something holy about returning to the breath.

I have lived through seasons when I couldn't catch my own breath, when grief knocked the wind out of me. Trauma made me feel unsafe in my own body. Anxiety sped up my breathing and left me ungrounded.

But God gently invited me back to the breath He gave me through reading the Scriptures.

When I feel lost, afraid, or numb, I remember I can begin again... with a single inhale.

Breath has become my reset button.

Sometimes my prayer has no words, just deep, mindful breathing while my soul catches up to my body.

Sometimes it's a quiet sigh that says, "God, I don't have the words right now... but I know You are near." Through my breath, I worship.

And that is sacred.

# Reflection Prompt

Take a moment to be still. Close your eyes.

Check in with your breath.

1. Is it shallow, rushed, or calm?

_______________________________________________

_______________________________________________

2. When was the last time you paused just to breathe?

_______________________________________________

_______________________________________________

3. What emotions begin to stir when you give your breath your full attention?

_______________________________________________

_______________________________________________

*Let this moment become sacred. Let your body speak and your soul gently listen. You are not behind. You are just one breath away from peace.*

# Try This

---

*The 4-7-8 Breath*

When you feel anxious, disconnected, or overwhelmed, try this gentle breathwork:

1. Inhale for 4 seconds

   Feel the breath enter like fresh grace.

2. Hold for 7 seconds

   Let the stillness surround you like divine peace.

3. Exhale for 8 seconds

   Release what no longer belongs to you. Sigh if you need to.
   Repeat 3–4 times.
   Whisper this as you breathe:
   "Your breath is in me, Lord. I am alive."
   "And You are always with me."

# Word for the Soul

Breath is holy.

It is not weakness to pause. It is worship. It is trust. Every inhale is a quiet miracle, a sacred reminder that God is still giving you life, moment by moment.

When you feel like you can't do anything else... breathe.

When the words won't come... breathe.

When the world feels loud and heavy... breathe.

Your breath is not just survival.

It is your sacred access point to peace, presence, and God's Spirit living within you.

# Notes & Reflections

# Practice 2
# The Practice of Faith

*"Now faith is confidence in what we hope for and assurance*
*about what we do not see."*
*— Hebrews 11:1 (NIV)*

Faith is not about knowing how everything will unfold, it is trusting that there is a Divine hand guiding it, even when you can't see the path.

For those who have lived through trauma, faith can feel foreign or even fragile. When life has taught you that safety and stability can vanish without warning, trusting again takes courage.

Yet faith is the bridge between despair and hope.

It's choosing to believe that healing is possible, even when your heart still aches. Faith doesn't erase pain; it gives pain a purpose.

It whispers, "You are not alone in this. There is a plan unfolding, even when you cannot yet see it."

Faith reminds us that what feels invisible is often the most powerful, such as love, peace, and the quiet strength that rises from within.

Faith invites us to rest, not in what we can control, but in who is holding us. When we dare to believe in what we cannot see, we make space for the unseen to become real within us and around us.

# Story Time

In Chapter 3 of my memoir, I share how I grew up in chaos, abuse, and silence. But at seventeen, I planned to find God after my birthday because I sensed that faith could lead me to peace.

The summer before I turned eighteen, I told my boyfriend that when my birthday came, I would have to break up with him. When he asked why, I couldn't give a clear answer, only that I needed to find God.

I hadn't grown up in church, but somehow, I knew there was more to life than what I was living. Deep down, I sensed that a relationship with God could lead me somewhere peaceful, somewhere safe.

By the end of that year, I followed through. I ended the relationship and found myself surrounded by godly women. Women who prayed, believed, and loved differently. They invited me to church, shared their stories of faith, and showed me what joy looked like when it came from God.

I didn't want to mimic their outward appearance; I wanted their peace. It was that hunger for peace that taught me how to separate myself from people, places, and things that did not reflect God's presence.

By faith, I believed that I too could experience the peace that "surpasses all understanding."

Over thirty years later, I still practice my faith daily. Not because of fear or rules, but because my heart has witnessed God's faithfulness over and over again. My faith is built not just on what He has done, but on what I know He is able to do.

Through every storm, my faith reminds me: no matter what comes or what goes, God remains.

# Reflection Prompt

Pause and ask yourself gently:

1. What do I believe about God?

___________________________________________________

___________________________________________________

2. What role has faith played in my survival?

___________________________________________________

___________________________________________________

3. Am I willing to explore faith in God, even if I am not sure what I believe?

___________________________________________________

___________________________________________________

*Let this moment become sacred. Even if all you can write is, "I don't know how, but I trust You." That counts. That's faith too.*

# Try This

*Faith in Practice*

1. Attend a church, meditation group, or spiritual gathering this week.
2. Read one Psalm each day for 7 days and write down one word or phrase that comforts you.
3. Write a letter to God (even if you're unsure what to say). Let honesty be your prayer.
4. Sit in silence and ask, "God, are You here? Will You help me heal?"
5. Create a faith jar. Write down moments where you've seen God show up, no matter how small. Revisit it when doubt comes.

# Word for the Soul

You don't need perfect faith to begin healing, just a willing heart. God meets you in the middle of your doubt, your questions, and your pain.

Faith isn't about being strong enough; it's about trusting the One who is. Even when your vision is clouded, God is still moving.

You are not alone.

You never were.

Faith invites you to surrender what you cannot fix and to rest in what you cannot yet see. It teaches your heart to breathe again and to believe that something sacred is forming in the unseen places.

Every time you choose hope over fear, you strengthen your spiritual muscles. And when your faith wavers, remember this:

Even a mustard seed can move mountains.

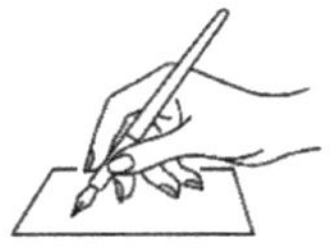

# Notes & Reflections

PRACTICE 3

# THE PRACTICE OF PRAYER

🌱

*"Pray without ceasing."*
*— 1 Thessalonians 5:17 (KJV)*

At first glance, "pray without ceasing" might sound impossible. But it's not about praying nonstop with perfect words, it's about staying connected to God throughout your day.

To pray continually is to invite God into everything:

> Into the silent moments
> Into the messiness
> Into the stuck, confused, or weary places

It is letting your life become a living prayer.

When you don't have the words, your tears can speak. When your strength is gone, your stillness can hold space for God.

Prayer isn't always loud, it's often a whisper, a breath, or a quiet "thank You." Sometimes, it's just the awareness: God, You are here with me.

"Pray without ceasing" is not a demand, it's an invitation to stay close.

And staying close is how we begin to get unstuck.

# Story Time

In Chapter 9 of my memoir, I describe the beginning of my healing. Prayer became my bridge from despair to hope. It has been my lifeline, not just in church pews or quiet corners, but in the messy middle of real life.

When I was on the edge of breaking down in my spirit and my soul, prayer carried me. Not the kind of prayer that's polished or profound. It's the kind that weeps behind the wheel, whispers under your breath, or simply pleads, "Jesus, help me."

For a long time, I thought prayer had to sound powerful. That it had to be eloquent. Then I remembered what the disciples asked Jesus:

*"Lord, teach us to pray." (Luke 11:1)*

That request freed me. It reminded me, prayer is learned. It grows as we grow. And sometimes, all you have is a one-word cry in the middle of chaos.

That still counts.

When I feel stuck emotionally, mentally, or spiritually, prayer becomes my bridge over troubled waters. It carries me from my overthinking headspace back into the peace of God's presence. It's there I remember:

> I'm not walking alone.
> I don't need all the answers.
> I just need to stay connected.

I've learned to pray without ceasing by praying while walking, while crying, while cooking, while simply sitting in silence.

I talk to God throughout the day. Not with pressure, but with presence.

And that's how I get unstuck.

# Reflection Prompt

Pause and ask yourself gently:

1. Where in my life do I feel stuck emotionally, mentally, or spiritually?

_______________________________________________

_______________________________________________

2. What might be holding me back from praying about it?

_______________________________________________

_______________________________________________

3. What would it look like to give God full access to that stuck place?

_______________________________________________

_______________________________________________

*Let this moment become sacred. God honors your honesty more than He expects eloquence.*

# **Try This**

---

*Turning Stuck into Prayer*

1. Name the Stuck Place

   Grab a journal or whisper it in your heart.
   Speak the heaviness aloud.

2. Turn It into a One-Line Prayer

   "God, I feel stuck, and I don't know what to do."
   "Lord, soften the fear I'm carrying."
   "Jesus, just be near."

3. Come Back to It Throughout the Day

   Repeat your sentence prayer while walking, cooking, driving.
   Let it become your steady rhythm of returning to God.

4. Let Silence Be a Prayer Too

   God hears what you don't say.
   Your stillness is sacred space.
   He'll meet you in the quiet.

# Word for the Soul

Prayer isn't a performance, it's permission.

Permission to be honest.

To be tired.

To not have it all together.

God isn't asking for perfect words, He's inviting you to be present. And the more you talk to Him, the more you'll find your way forward.

You don't have to unstick yourself in your own strength. Just open your mouth or your heart and He will meet you there.

You are heard.

You are held.

You are healing.

# Notes & Reflections

# PRACTICE 4
# THE PRACTICE OF MEDITATION

*"Keep this Book of the Law always on your lips; meditate on it day
and night, so that you may be careful to do everything written in it.
Then you will be prosperous and successful."*
*—Joshua 1:8 (NIV)*

You don't have to strive for clarity, it unfolds in stillness.

When you meditate on God's Word, you're not just reading ancient text, you're opening yourself to a living conversation with a present God.

To meditate day and night means to reflect deeply and consistently on what God has spoken.

It's more than memorization, it's transformation. It's allowing God's truth to settle into your spirit, reshape your thoughts, and guide your path.

Meditating "day and night" symbolizes consistency, not just a once-a-week or every-now-and-then moment, but a daily rhythm of returning to truth.

When we slow down to meditate, we make room for wisdom, guidance, and inner peace to rise.

We stop reacting and start receiving.

Meditation isn't passivity, it's stillness. And stillness is sacred listening that opens your awareness to purpose.

# Story Time

In Chapter 6 of my memoir, I share how I asked God if I should marry my first husband, but I didn't wait for His answer.

There was a time in my life when I would spend hours in the Scriptures. I memorized them. I wrote them down. I shared them with others.

But I hadn't yet learned how to meditate on them.

I was quick to research a verse or repeat it to someone else, but I rarely paused long enough to ask God, "What are You really saying to me?"

I skipped over the silence.

Before I married my first husband, I asked the Lord if I should marry him. I prayed. I searched the Scriptures. I even found a verse that seemed to align with what I wanted, and I took that as confirmation.

But I didn't wait in stillness. I didn't make space for God's deeper voice.

Had I paused and meditated, I would have heard, "Don't marry him." I would have realized he only married because I was pregnant. Meditation would've shown me that I was trying to convince myself of something God never said.

Since then, I've learned the sacred art of silence and the deep revelation it carries.

Meditation has taught me patience.

It's no longer about rushing to act. Now, I sit. I breathe. I let the Word rest in me. Meditation opens space for divine discovery of who God is, who I am, and where I am being led.

If you're searching for direction, identity, or clarity, don't rush. Don't strive. Just sit with God in stillness.

That's where revelation lives.

# Reflection Prompt

Take a moment to reflect on the times you've searched for answers and moved too quickly.

Journal your response to one or more of the following:

1. What decisions have I made based on what I wanted to hear, rather than what God was really saying?

_______________________________________________

_______________________________________________

2. How has the absence of stillness affected my clarity and peace?

_______________________________________________

_______________________________________________

3. What might God reveal if I gave Him room to speak?

_______________________________________________

_______________________________________________

*Let this moment become sacred. Allow yourself to write, cry, release, or simply receive.*
*Stillness isn't empty, it's expectant.*

# Try This

---

*Meditating on Scripture*

1. Choose One Verse

    Pick a scripture you've heard before and approach it slowly and openly.

    (Example: Psalm 46:10 – "Be still and know that I am God.").

2. Read Slowly

    Read it out loud once. Then again. Let each word settle.

3. Sit in Silence

    Set a timer for 5–10 minutes. Close your eyes. Breathe deeply.

    (If your mind wanders, gently return to the verse).

4. Ask One Gentle Question

    "God, what are You revealing to me here?"

    (Then... wait. No fixing. No forcing. Just be).

5. Write What You Hear or Feel

    Capture any words, feelings, or images.

    You are learning to listen with your heart.

# Word for the Soul

Meditation is not about emptying your mind; it's about making room.

Room for peace.

Room for truth.

Room for God's whisper.

In the stillness, you become more aware of His nearness.

In the quiet, He clarifies what chaos tried to confuse. You don't have to strive for answers; you just have to sit with the One who holds them.

God is not far. He is waiting in the stillness.

And so much can be revealed... when you finally get quiet enough to listen.

# Notes & Reflections

# PART TWO

# EXPRESSIVE PRACTICES

*Giving your story a voice, your body a choice, and*
*your healing a way forward.*
**—Amanda D. Ligon**

PRACTICE 5

# THE PRACTICE OF WALKING

*"Even though I walk through the darkest valley, I will fear no evil, for You are with*
*me; Your rod and Your staff, they comfort me."*
**— Psalm 23:4 (NIV)**

Walking is more than movement; it's medicine for the soul.

Psalm 23:4 acknowledges a tender truth: life will lead us through valleys. Dark ones. Lonely ones. Confusing ones.

The valley might look like grief, trauma, betrayal, depression, fear, or despair. But even in the valley, it's only a shadow. And where there is shadow... there is also Light.

This verse reminds us that we do not walk alone. God is with us, guiding, protecting, and comforting us every step of the way.

Whatever feels like your darkest valley, know this:

> It doesn't have the final word
> It is not forever
> You are not stuck
> And you are not walking it alone

To walk through the valley is to move in faith. It's courage in motion. And each step becomes an act of trust. Trust that you are going somewhere sacred, even if you don't see the full map yet.

Walking is how we move forward through loss, through waiting, through questions, and into peace.

# Story Time

In Chapter 9 of my memoir, I describe how leaving is the first step. That first step isn't just physical, it is spiritual.

Walking has always been my go-to. I've walked to release stress, to lose weight, to find clarity, and to reconnect with God and nature. When the world feels too loud, too heavy, or too tight, I lace up and walk it out. Sometimes I don't know where I'm walking to. I just know I need to walk away from pressure, from noise, from overwhelm. Eventually, I pause... breathe... and turn around to walk the same path home. This time with a little less weight and a little more peace.

I often walk with music or an uplifting message in my ears, but many times, I walk in complete silence.

And it's in that silence, step by step that I begin to release what had me tangled up.

My breath slows.

My mind unclenches.

My shoulders soften.

And something sacred happens.

By the time I return home, I either:

> Accept what I cannot change and surrender it to God, or
> Receive a fresh insight, a gentle solution, or the courage to respond differently.

I've been walking through pain since I was a little girl. And under the open sky, I embrace:

I am alive.
I am moving.
I am healing.
And God walks with me.

# Reflection Prompt

Walking is good for the mind, heart, and soul.

1. Where do your feet take you when your heart feels heavy?

2. This week, set aside time for a walk. No agenda. No need to perform. Just be present. Listen to music or let silence guide you. Pray, cry, or breathe deeply. Walk until you feel tired or until something in you feels lighter. Share your experience. How was it?

3. As you walk, what is a simple, one-sentence prayer you can repeat with each step? (For example: *"God, Thank You for being with me." "Casting all my cares upon You Lord."*) Reflect on how this rhythm of prayer and movement settles your spirit.

*Let this moment become sacred. Your movement is a prayer. Let your pen be the echo.*

# **Try This**

---

*Walk It Out*

During your next walk, speak this softly over yourself:

> I walk with purpose.
> I walk with peace.
> I walk with understanding.
> God walks with me.

Bonus Tips:

> Stay hydrated, bring water with you.
> Stretch before and after your walk to honor your body.
> Let your walk be about connection, not destination.

Even five minutes of movement can open space for clarity and healing.

# Word for the Soul

Movement is one of the most sacred ways to regulate the nervous system. When you walk, your body finds rhythm: Left foot. Right foot. Inhale. Exhale. And that rhythm speaks safety to your soul.

Walking in nature only deepens the healing.

The wind, the sunlight, the trees, the sky, each one whispers: You are alive. You are guided. You are held.

Walking isn't just about getting somewhere; it's about processing what your body was never meant to carry alone.

Let your steps be sacred.

Let the path hold your pain.

Let the air remind you: You are not walking this alone.

God is beside you. The valley is not forever. Keep walking... There is peace ahead.

# Notes & Reflections

# PRACTICE 6
# THE PRACTICE OF WRITING

*"Write the vision and make it plain on tablets, so that*
*whoever reads it may run with it."*
**— Habakkuk 2:2 (NIV)**

This scripture reminds us that writing isn't just for remembering, it's for releasing, revealing, and running toward what's next.

Journaling is how we give our pain a name, our dreams a place to live, and our healing a voice.

Some pain isn't meant to be tucked away or explained, it's meant to be released.

That's what journaling becomes: a container for your truth, a soft place for your rage, and a private witness to your healing.

When you write, you don't just express...

You exhale.

And the verse doesn't end there. We write so that others "may run with it." This is the promise hidden inside our pain.

The story you are afraid to write is the very story someone else needs to read to find the courage to run their own race.

Your words, written plainly and honestly on the tablet of your heart and your journal, can become the fuel for someone else's freedom.

Writing is not just an act of personal healing; it is an act of communal hope.

# Story Time

Chapter 8 of my memoir is the result of years of writing my way through trauma. I wrote to remember, to release, and to reclaim my voice. Writing became the sacred practice that helped me speak the unspeakable.

When you've experienced deep pain, so much lingers under the surface, waiting to be seen, spoken, and released. But the hard truth is, not everyone is meant to hear it. And not everyone is safe enough to hold it.

Some people turn away. Others shut down. And some try to fix what was never theirs to fix.

I began to realize I couldn't keep emotionally dumping onto family or friends, especially when they weren't equipped to hold the weight of my truth.

Sometimes I would start sharing, and the conversation would shift. Some would change the subject. Others would meet my pain with their own.

So, I did something simple:

I went to the store. Bought a notebook. And gave myself permission to write it out.

I didn't care about grammar. I didn't worry about spelling or punctuation. I just picked up a pen... and poured.

Whatever came to mind, I let it land on the page.

I wrote every day without judgment. And over time, I noticed something beautiful:

I was lighter.

I was stronger.

I was finding peace one page at a time.

Yes, there are moments when we need to talk to someone. But in the in-between, when I couldn't reach a therapist or didn't want to burden anyone, journaling became my safe place. It became my lifeline. And the more I wrote, the more I healed.

Eventually... I wrote until it became a book.

# **Reflection Prompt**

There is freedom in being fully and fearlessly honest.

1. What is your heart holding that's asking to be released?



2. What loss have you experienced that your soul still carries?



3. What pain have you tried to outrun or numb?



4. What dream or story is still inside you waiting to be born?



*Let this moment become sacred. Let the page hold what your body no longer needs to carry. Write like no one is watching. Write messy. Write true.*

# Try This

*Let Your Fingers Speak*

Writing allows the mind and heart to make room.

1. Begin with this gentle declaration:

> My words are worthy.
> My feelings matter.
> I release what no longer serves me.
> I write my truth and heal in the process.

2. Reflect on these journal prompts:

> If I could write about the "stuck" version of me, what would I say?
> What did that version of me teach me about God, about myself, and about my strength?

Let your writing be a conversation between your past and your healing.

3. This week, write a letter that you never intend to send. It could be to your younger self, to someone who hurt you, to a part of you that feels lost, or even to God. Don't worry about grammar or making sense. Just pour your unfiltered thoughts, feelings, anger, grief, or gratitude onto the page(s). When you are finished, you can keep it, shred it, or safely burn it as a symbol of release. Notice the freedom that comes from speaking your truth without fear of judgment.

4. For the next seven days, begin or end your day by writing down three specific things you are grateful for. They don't have to be big. Perhaps it's the warmth of your morning coffee, a song that lifted your spirit, or the strength it took to get out of bed. On the final day, read your list of 21 items aloud. Let this practice be a gentle anchor, grounding you in the goodness that still exists, even on the hardest days.

# Word for the Soul

When we journal, we move from chaos to clarity. From bottled-up emotion to breath. From silence to healing.

Journaling doesn't require perfect grammar or spelling; it just requires honesty.

It makes the invisible visible. It gives your nervous system a place to exhale. Journaling is a trauma-informed tool that creates safety for your mind and body. It holds space for your truth without interruption, without judgment.

It can become:

A prayer on paper
A sacred altar of remembrance
A mirror that reflects how far you've come

Looking back at old entries allows you to see the evidence:

You've grown. You've healed. You've survived. You are not who you used to be.

And your story deserves to be seen first by you. Write as if God is reading alongside you.

Because He is. And He is not ashamed of your story.

He is helping you write the next chapter.

# Notes & Reflections

# THE PRACTICE OF CREATING

*"See, I am doing a new thing! Now it springs up; do you not
perceive it? I am making a way in the wilderness and streams
in the wasteland."*
**— Isaiah 43:19 (NIV)**

This scripture is God's declaration of hope in hidden places.

Even when we feel lost, broken, or barren, God is still doing something new.

He's making a way in places that once felt closed. He's releasing streams in spaces that felt dry. He's restoring joy in hearts that forgot how to feel it.

Creativity allows us to partner with that newness. To make space for beauty to rise from the rubble. To paint, write, sing, or move our way toward joy.

Not to impress, but to remember how to live again.

This verse invites you to perceive what God is birthing, even if it starts small.

Creativity becomes the spiritual practice of noticing and joining God in the act of renewal.

In its purest form, creativity is a practice of perception. It is training our eyes to see what God is doing.

When you arrange flowers in a vase, bake bread for a neighbor, or choose a colorful scarf to wear, you are not just making something; you are making a declaration of faith.

You are telling the truth that beauty can exist alongside brokenness. And you are partnering with the God who makes streams in the desert and who is, at this very moment, doing a new thing in you.

# Story Time

In Chapter 10 of my memoir, I share how I relocated with my children to break the cycle of abuse. Relocating to break the toxic cycle of abuse was a brave and necessary move, but it came with a heavy stillness. I had my children, yes, but no friends nearby. No family. No familiar streets. Just freedom... and loneliness.

The days began to blur. We didn't know where the parks were or where to find the best pizza spot. Even the freeways felt like a maze. The silence started to settle into our bones, and I could feel the emotional weight in my home.

So, I got creative.

I took the kids to a local craft store and bought the basics: canvases, paintbrushes, and vibrant paints. When we got home, we laid towels across the floor, turned on soft, joyful music, and followed a beginner YouTube tutorial just to do something together.

And just like that, we began to paint.

There were silly strokes, "oops" moments, surprising bursts of color, and so much laughter. But most of all, there was presence.

We weren't just killing time.

We were reconnecting.

We were healing.

We were creating joy.

In that moment, creativity became more than an activity. It became a form of survival. A soft ritual. A sacred reset.

Sometimes creativity looks like painting. Other times, it's rearranging your living room to shift energy. It could be writing on the back of a receipt, cooking something new, or humming a made-up song in the shower.

It doesn't have to be big.

It just has to be.

# Reflection Prompt

Joy is allowed here.

1. What's one creative outlet that helped you feel grounded in a hard season?

2. If you haven't explored one yet, what's something you've always wanted to try, no matter how small, simple, or silly?

3. Is it drawing, dancing, planting, baking, sewing, writing, decorating, or singing?

*Let this moment become sacred. Let it be imperfect, playful, and freeing.*

# Try This

---

*Creative Affirmation*

Allow your creativity to guide you this week.

1. Speak this over yourself:

> I create because I am created.
> My imagination is sacred.
> My expression is healing.
> There is no right way, just the brave way.
> I am allowed to be messy, magical, and made new.

2. Then ask yourself:

> If I gave myself creative permission, what would I try?
> What's one way I can honor my inner artist this week?

3. Set a timer for five minutes. In that time, create something with no goal other than the act of creating itself. Grab a pen and doodle on a napkin. Hum a new melody into your phone's voice recorder. Rearrange a few items on a shelf to make a small corner of your room feel more beautiful. This isn't about making a masterpiece; it's about making space for your spirit to play. How does it feel to create without pressure?

4. Create a short playlist of 3-5 songs that feel like medicine to your soul. One song that helps you grieve, one that brings joy, one that makes you feel strong, one that helps you rest, and one that feels like pure hope. Title the playlist "My Healing," and listen to it this week when you need to reconnect with yourself. Music is a powerful way to create a healing environment for your heart.

# Word for the Soul

Creativity gently rewires the nervous system. It shifts us out of survival mode and into connection mode. It reminds our bodies that beauty still exists, and joy is still accessible. When you create, you're not escaping life, you're reclaiming it.

Whether it's painting, planting, dancing, cooking, decorating, or journaling, creative expression becomes your personal sanctuary.

It becomes a soft reminder:

"I am still here.
I still have beauty in me.
I still get to shape something with my own hands."
Creativity isn't just for artists; it's for anyone who's ever needed to exhale pain, rediscover joy, or remember they're still becoming.

You don't need a canvas or a title.
You just need a little space… and permission.
You are a divine creation.
Let what's in you create something new.

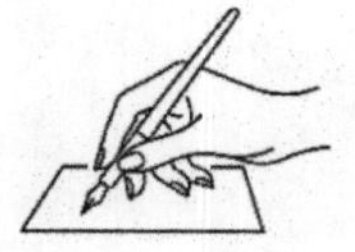

# Notes & Reflections

# THE PRACTICE OF SINGING

*"Sing to the Lord a new song, for He has done marvelous things…"*
**— Psalm 98:1 (NIV)**

There are certain sounds that open the heart and melodies that reach places words cannot. Singing has always been more than music; it's medicine.

Psalm 98:1 isn't just about singing a song; it's about offering God a *new* song. Not because He seeks perfection… but because He delights in presence.

Your new song might rise after heartbreak. It might come through tears. It might sound different than before, but it's still worship.

Singing and humming become sacred acts of remembrance.

They remind us of what God has done and what He's still doing. They invite us into hope, healing, and harmony—even in our brokenness.

And the best part?

God isn't asking for perfect pitch. He's asking for a present heart.

A "new song" is any sound that breaks the silence of pain imposed on you. It can be a hummed melody when anxiety is high, a whispered chorus in the car, or a full-throated anthem of praise for the "marvelous things" He has done.

The greatest of things is that you are still here, and your voice is returning.

# Story Time

In Chapter 8 of my memoir, I share how healing begins the moment silence loses its grip on your voice. During those dark seasons when I felt stuck, singing old hymns of the Christian church became my therapy.

In my first marriage, I was so lonely and depressed. I was going to church... but I was going through it.

One Friday evening, I picked someone up on the way to church service. As we drove, we started talking about what song to sing for testimony service. She mentioned one I'd never heard: "When I See Jesus, Amen."

She sang it softly in the car, and by the time we pulled up to the church, I had learned the chorus. During the service, I stood nervous, heavy, worn down, and sang what I could remember:

*"When I see Jesus, Amen*
*When I see Jesus, Amen*
*When I see Jesus... all of my loneliness,*
*All of my sadness,*
*All of my depression will be over...*
*When I see Jesus, Amen."*

Tears came, and so did relief.

I didn't need to hit every note. I just needed to show up with my voice. And in that moment, my voice became my healing. What I didn't know then was that singing that song became my therapy.

Those old hymns didn't just fill the room; they carried my soul when my body was tired and my mind was weary.

I felt Held.

I felt Heard.

And I felt Lighter.

Singing touched something deep in me. It didn't come from me; it came through me. And I've never forgotten what that melody unlocked in my spirit.

# Reflection Prompt

Reflect on one or more of these:

1. What song carried me through a hard season?

2. What does my body feel like after I sing or hum?

3. If I could sing a song to the younger me, what would it be?

*Let this moment become sacred. Allow your voice to reconnect you with your soul.*

# **Try This**

---

*Sing and Hum for Healing*

Your voice is therapeutic.

Sing a song that reminds you of who God is or who you are.

Hum softly to yourself when anxiety rises.

Create a playlist that feels like hope, healing, or survival.

Sing in the shower, in the car, or while you walk. No performance needed.

Let your voice become your refuge.

Whether it's a whisper, a hum, or a hallelujah, let your sound rise.

# Word for the Soul

Singing and humming do more than lift the spirit, they literally regulate the nervous system. They stimulate the vagus nerve, calm the heart rate, and release feel-good hormones like dopamine and oxytocin.

Old hymns carry emotional memories. When you sing what your ancestors sang, you tap into the resilience that ran through their bones. You join a chorus of survival. Of sacred memory.

Hum through heartbreak. Hum through the silence. Hum when words won't come. Even if it's just one soft note repeated over and over. Let your hum be a prayer. Let your song be a sound of resistance and rest.

You don't need a perfect voice.
You just need a present heart.
So, when the tears fall... hum.
When anxiety rises... hum.
When the silence is heavy... let your voice rise like incense.
Your voice—cracked, quiet, trembling, or loud is sacred.
You are still here. And your voice still matters.

# Notes & Reflections

## PART THREE

# RESTORATIVE PRACTICES

*Mending the broken places with gentleness, grace,*
*and the courage to receive.*
*—Amanda D. Ligon*

# Practice 9
# The Practice of Cold Water

*"When you pass through the waters, I will be with you."*
*— Isaiah 43:2 (NIV)*

Water has always been symbolic in Scripture; of chaos, transition, baptism, and breakthrough.

But this verse doesn't say *if* you pass through the waters. It says *when*.

Because hard seasons are guaranteed. Waters will rise. Emotions will flood. Life will shake you. Yet through it all, God promises to be with you.

Cold water, specifically, is both physical and symbolic. It awakens. It resets. It reminds you that you're still here.

Cold water doesn't take away the pain, but it offers presence. It grounds your body in the now, shifts your nervous system, and reintroduces you to your strength.

This verse is a divine assurance:

Even in discomfort, you are not abandoned.

Even in the coldest moments, God is in the water with you.

Cold water becomes a sacred practice of resilience and renewal.

# Story Time

In Chapter 7 of my memoir, I shared how my body never forgot what my mind tried to erase.

I didn't learn about the vagus nerve until adulthood. I didn't know cold water could regulate the nervous system, lower anxiety, or ground you in the present. I just knew that growing up in a crowded apartment with twelve cousins, one bathroom, and a single hot water tank, you either got in early, or you got in cold.

And most days, I got in cold.

At the time, I thought I was just surviving. But looking back, I see it.

Cold water was my initiation into resilience. I hated it at first. But after each shower, I felt... different. Awake. Alive. Empowered. Like I had done something hard and come out stronger.

Even now, when life feels heavy or I sense myself spiraling, I step into a cold shower. Not to punish myself, but to return to myself.

Cold water met me in moments when I was ready to give up.

It has now become a kind of baptism, a ritual of remembrance:

I've been through worse.

I'm still here.

Each time I choose to connect with myself in cold water, I'm choosing the truth: the discomfort won't drown me.

I come out standing—clearer, calmer, and a little more convinced that resilience lives in my body. And God is always with me even in cold water.

# Reflection Prompt

Take a deep breath and reflect:

1. When have I felt empowered after doing something uncomfortable?

2. What happens in my body before and after I engage with cold water?

3. Could cold water become a ritual of renewal for me?

*Let this moment become sacred. Allow your reflection to become a way of reclaiming your strength.*

# Try This

---

*Simple Cold-Water Practices*

Start where you are. Listen to your body. Choose one of the following:

1. Cold shower: End your regular shower with 30 seconds of cold water. Increase slowly.
2. Cold face rinse: Splash cold water on your face for 10–20 seconds to ground your body.
3. Cold water bowl: Dip your face or hands into a bowl of ice water for emotional reset.
4. Cold compress: Apply to your chest, neck, or wrists during moments of overwhelm.

These small practices can signal to your nervous system:

- You are safe.
- You are supported.
- You are still standing.

# Word for the Soul

Cold water doesn't just wake you up; it reminds you of who you are.

It activates the vagus nerve, calming anxiety and helping you shift from chaos to clarity.

It slows your heart rate, deepens your breath, and brings you back into the present moment.

It boosts your mood by releasing endorphins and dopamine, creating a natural sense of relief.

Cold water is sacred. Not because it is easy, but because it is honest. You won't always have warm comfort. But you will always have the choice to return to your breath. To your body. To the presence of God. Even when the water feels cold.

You are not powerless. You are not drowning. You've survived the waters before.
And with every drop that touches your skin, you'll remember:
You are still here.
And you are not alone.

# Notes & Reflections

# THE PRACTICE OF CONNECTION

*"Let us not give up meeting together, as some are in the habit
of doing, but encouraging one another..."*
**— Hebrews 10:25 (NIV)**

There are times when isolation feels easier. When silence feels safer than explaining your pain and when it seems like nobody would understand anyway.

But Scripture reminds us: don't stop connecting. We weren't created to survive alone.

This verse isn't just about gathering in a building; it's about gathering hearts.

It's about encouraging one another when life gets heavy. Showing up in presence, in prayer, in phone calls, and in small ways that whisper: "You are not alone."

Connection is not a luxury. It's not a weakness.

It is medicine.

It is God's design for restoration.

When you share your story, your laughter, your grief, or your joy, you make space for healing to happen... for both of you.

Healing moves faster when love has a witness.

# Story Time

In Chapter 10 of my memoir, I describe the safe people who helped me break the cycle of abuse. Before anyone could help me, I had to believe that I was worthy, I was loved, and I could end the cycle of abuse.

I'll never forget the day my grandmother called me out of the blue and asked softly:

"Are you okay?"

She said she had been feeling something in her spirit, that something wasn't sitting right. I hesitated... but I told her the truth. I had left my home in the middle of the night. Pregnant. Alone. Walking for my safety.

I will never forget the way her voice broke:

"Baby, I have a car. You never have to walk when I have a car. You could've called me. I would've come and gotten you, day or night."

Her words poured love into me. That call reminded me of something I had forgotten:

I was loved by my grandmother. And I didn't have to carry it all alone.

After the divorce, I began realizing how many people had truly cared about me all along; family, friends, people I had unintentionally distanced myself from during the darkest seasons.

So, I started reaching back out. Not just when I was hurting...

But when I was healing. When I was celebrating a small win. When I had good news. When I just wanted to laugh about something silly. And something began to shift inside me:

The more I connected, the more connected I felt to them, yes... But also, to myself.

# Reflection Prompt

Gently reflect on these:

1. Who do I miss, but haven't reached out to in a while?

_______________________________________________

_______________________________________________

2. What kind of connection does my soul long for right now?

_______________________________________________

_______________________________________________

3. What's one small, brave step I can take to receive or offer that connection?

_______________________________________________

_______________________________________________

*Let this moment become sacred. You are worthy of reaching out and being reached for.*

# Try This

---



*Intentionally Connect This Week*

Choose one small act of reconnection:

1. Call someone just to check in, no agenda.
2. Send a voice note instead of a text, let them hear your heart.
3. Share something you are grateful for or a small win.
4. Invite someone to walk, talk, or pray with you.
5. Let someone know you miss them, even if it's been years.
6. Respond to someone who has reached out to you. If they are a safe person, let them in.

Sometimes the healing begins not in what you say, but in simply showing up.

# Word for the Soul

You don't have to walk this road alone.

There are people who would stop what they're doing just to remind you: You matter. You don't have to wait for the next crisis to call. You can reach out in joy. You can reach out in silence. You can reach out in healing.

Because connection isn't just emotional; it's spiritual. It rewires the nervous system. It regulates the heart.

It reminds your soul:

You are seen.
You are needed.
You are never too much or too late.
Call when you're hurting.
Call when you're happy.
Call just because you want to hear a familiar voice.

Because sometimes the greatest miracle isn't being rescued... It's remembering you were never alone in the first place.

# Notes & Reflections

# Practice 11
# The Practice of Healthcare

*"It is not the healthy who need a doctor, but the sick."*
*— Luke 5:31 (NIV)*

In this verse, Jesus speaks to the deeper need for spiritual healing, but the truth still echoes into the physical:

Being unwell is not a sign of failure; it's a call for care.

God is the Ultimate Healer, but He also works through people—through doctors, nurses, nutritionists, and counselors. Healthcare professionals are extensions of God's compassion.

Sometimes we carry pain for so long, it becomes background noise:

The fatigue.
The tight chest.
The headaches.
The anxiety we call "just stress."

We normalize it. We power through it. We minimize it. But what if those symptoms aren't nuisances to silence, but divine signals asking to be heard?

Our bodies don't lie. They speak. And when we listen, we heal.

Caring for your body is one of the most sacred ways to honor the life God breathed into you.

# Story Time

In Chapter 11 of my memoir, I describe how I learned that healing is holistic—it involves the body, mind, and spirit. Connecting with healthcare professionals became part of my sacred healing journey.

There was a time in my life when I would push through headaches, exhaustion, and anxiety, all in the name of responsibility.

I was a mother.

I was working.

I was serving at church.

I told myself, "This is what strong women do." And I kept pushing.

Until one day, the pain stopped me.

My headache was pounding so loudly, I couldn't move.

My youngest child had to call 911, and I was rushed to the hospital. What I thought was "just stress" turned out that my blood pressure and sodium levels were dangerously high. My body was waving a white flag, screaming what I had been ignoring.

That day changed me.

I learned that ignoring pain doesn't prove strength, it postpones healing. And worse... that it teaches our children that their bodies don't matter either. We can't model self-abandonment and expect our children to honor their own needs.

Getting help isn't a weakness.

It is wisdom.
It is parenting.
It is legacy.
And it is love.

# Reflection Prompt

Take a moment and ask:

1. What is my body trying to tell me right now?

_________________________________________________

_________________________________________________

2. What appointment or check-up have I been putting off?

_________________________________________________

_________________________________________________

3. What message am I passing to others, especially children about honoring or ignoring their needs?

_________________________________________________

_________________________________________________

*Let this moment become sacred. Allow this to be a quiet commitment to care for your body, your future, and your family.*

# Try This

---

*Prepare for Your Next Appointment*

If you haven't had a check-up recently, schedule one and prepare like you're advocating for someone you love.

Before your visit:

1. Write down any symptoms, even small ones.
2. Note when they started and how often they occur.
3. List your current medications, supplements, or concerns.
4. Mention recent stressors or major changes.
5. Prepare 2–3 questions you want answered.
6. Ask for lab work, referrals, or follow-up.
7. Bring a trusted friend or written notes if you need support.
8. Don't be afraid to say: "Can you explain that again?"

You are not a burden.

You are a being.

And you deserve clear, compassionate care.

# Word for the Soul

---

Symptoms are signals.

Your body is not betraying you; it's begging you to listen. Whether it's therapy, bloodwork, medication, or rest... don't delay. You are too valuable to live untreated. Getting help isn't failure, it's stewardship.

Mental health is health.

It's okay to feel tired and not know why.
It's okay to cry in your car and still go to your session.
It's okay to take medication if that's part of your healing.
It's okay to say: "I don't feel like myself... and I want to understand why."

Pain is not the enemy. Neglect is.

Let every doctor's visit, every therapy session, every test or check-up be your declaration:

"I deserve to know what's going on inside me. And I give myself permission to heal."

# Notes & Reflections

# THE PRACTICE OF THERAPY

*"Where there is no counsel, the people fall; But in the*
*multitude of counselors there is safety."*
— ***Proverbs 11:14 (NKJV)***

This verse reminds us that guidance is not a weakness, it is a safeguard.

We were never meant to navigate life or healing alone. When we try to carry our pain by ourselves, we lose direction and strength.

But when we invite wise counsel into our journey—whether that's a friend, pastor, mentor, or licensed therapist, we find stability and safety.

The word counselors is plural for a reason.

Healing often happens in community.

God designed us for connection and shared wisdom. Therapy, coaching, and spiritual guidance are not replacements for faith; they are extensions of it.

Seeking therapy is an act of courage and belief: belief that God can use others to help us find healing and freedom.

Sometimes, God's answer to our prayer for help comes through another person's training, compassion, or insight. He places people along our path who carry the very wisdom we've been praying for. Accepting their help doesn't mean we lack faith; it means we're walking in it.

Seeking counsel is how we partner with God in our healing.

# Story Time

In Chapter 11 of my memoir, I shared how I spent over 86-months in trauma-informed therapy. Those sessions were sacred ground. They helped me dig safely into the roots of my trauma and begin to heal deeply.

For years, I believed I could heal myself. I prayed, read Scripture, and practiced spiritual disciplines. Eventually, I realized that I needed help beyond what I could do alone.

The trauma I carried—childhood sexual abuse, exploitation, and domestic violence—had roots buried deep. I needed someone trained to help me dig safely. It took time to find the right fit, but when I did, everything changed.

My trauma-informed therapist Ms. Lisa specialized in EMDR (Eye Movement Desensitization and Reprocessing), and for the first time, I felt safe to speak the unspeakable.

Week after week, I learned to regulate my nervous system, to grieve, to rest, and to breathe when I was subconsciously holding my breath. Some sessions I cried, some I was silent, often when each session was nearing the end, I was ready to run out the door, but I kept showing up.

I always scheduled and kept my appointment. Initially to see the therapist, then one day I began to see and hear myself.

That's what healing takes: showing up, again, and again, until your soul catches up with your hope.

Therapy didn't weaken my faith, it deepened it.

Prayer gave me hope; therapy gave me tools. Scripture anchored me in truth; together I began to heal.

God held me in His love, and my therapist helped me learn to hold myself with compassion.

Even now, as a Licensed Social Worker who supports others, I still seek therapy.

Because healing isn't a one-time event, it's a lifelong sacred practice.

# **Reflection Prompt**

---

Take a few quiet minutes to reflect:

1. What fears or beliefs have kept me from seeking counseling or support?

_______________________________________________

_______________________________________________

2. What would it mean to believe that therapy is an act of faith, not failure?

_______________________________________________

_______________________________________________

3. How might professional support help me heal more deeply?

_______________________________________________

_______________________________________________

---

*Let this moment become sacred. Your courage to seek help is the evidence of your hope.*

# Try This

---

*Taking the First Step*

Start here:

1.  Visit a therapy directory such as Psychology Today, Therapy for Black Girls, or Open Path Collective.
2.  Check out which therapist is in network under your health insurance provider.
3.  Ask your employer if they have an Employee Assistance Plan and if you can access a therapist.
4.  Read a few therapist profiles and note who resonates with you.
5.  Schedule a 15-minute consultation with at least one trauma-informed therapist.
6.  Prepare three questions to ask (for example: "How do you help trauma survivors feel safe?").
7.  Afterward, take a deep breath and notice how your body feels calm, hopeful, uneasy, curious.

Let that be your guide.

# Word for the Soul

Seeking therapy is not weakness, it's wisdom. It is honoring that some wounds are too deep to heal alone and that God works through the hearts and hands of counselors.

You deserve a space where you can speak the unspeakable, cry without apology, and remember without drowning.

Therapy gave me that space, and it can give you that space too. Those 86 months I spent in therapy were holy ground. They helped me rescue myself.

When life begins to feel heavy, I seek counsel. Because healing isn't a destination, it's a rhythm of returning to safety, again, and again. And asking for help isn't a failure; it's faith in motion.

God works through EMDR, CBT, somatic therapy, and every modality created to help His children heal. You don't have to do this alone; you were never meant to.

So, if you've been waiting for permission, here it is:

You are allowed to seek help.

You are allowed to take as long as you need.

You are allowed to find a therapist who truly sees you.

You are allowed to heal with support.

In an abundance of counselors, there is safety. And you deserve to be safe.

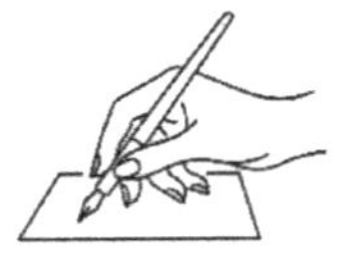

# Notes & Reflections

# PART FOUR

# TRANSFORMATIVE PRACTICES

*Becoming the person you were always meant to be —*
*healed, whole, and free.*
**—Amanda D. Ligon**

# THE PRACTICE OF GROWTH

*"Wisdom is the principal thing; therefore, get wisdom: and
with all thy getting get understanding."*
**— Proverbs 4:7 (KJV)**

Wisdom is not always born in peaceful places. Often, it comes from the wreckage. From the ending. From the ache.

This verse reminds us that wisdom is the priority, especially when life falls apart.

And with all our reaching for love, for comfort, for peace, for stability, for clarity, this Scripture says: *Get understanding.* Don't just get through it, learn something in it.

There will be seasons when everything familiar collapses:

> The job ends.
> The relationship dissolves.
> The routine disappears.
> A diagnosis is given.
> A loved one passes away.

Suddenly, you're left with silence and space. And in that space, it's tempting to reach for a quick fix:

> A shopping cart.
> A glass of wine.
> A text to the one you already let go.

But what if the discomfort isn't punishment? What if the pain is a portal?

Pain opens the door to deeper purpose, if we let it. When life strips you down, God may be inviting you into something new: a new lesson, a new level, a new you.

Loss creates space. And in that space, you get to choose what you plant:

Avoidance or understanding.
Bitterness or growth.
Wandering or wisdom.

# Story Time

In Chapter 10 of my memoir, I share how I had to learn to feel fully in order to heal deeply. I'll never forget the moment COVID hit and within three weeks my job was gone.

Just like that, I was unemployed. A single mother. Bills were due, rent to pay, kids to feed. No cushion. No backup. And there was no nearby family.

Panic tried to move in. I could've packed up and moved back to my home state. I could've given in to hopelessness. I could've told myself, "It's over. You missed your chance."

But I didn't.

I got quiet. I asked God, "Now what?" And the answer came quietly but clearly:

"Nothing will be wasted. Go back to grad school. Finish your degree."

At first, I doubted myself.

I didn't think I could finish solely online. I thought I was too old. Too far behind. Too tired. But I contacted the university's Master of Social Work program department. And in less than four weeks I was accepted and registered for autumn classes.

What I thought was an ending became a beginning.

Losing that job didn't destroy me, it developed me. It became proof that I was not too old, not too late, and not too lost.

I learned something powerful: I suffered loss—yet I survived.

And I didn't just survive, I graduated.

# Reflection Prompt

Reflect on your current or past season of stretching:

1. What has this painful moment revealed about me that peace never could?

2. Is there a subject I keep circling around, but have been afraid to fully face?

3. What wisdom is this season asking me to gather?

*Let this moment become sacred. You don't have to figure it all out today, just take the next brave step.*

# Try This

---

*Feed the Soil You Are In*

You don't have to transform overnight. Just water one seed at a time.

1. Take a free online course that lights a spark.
2. Learn a new skill, language, or healing practice.
3. Study the Word, not out of obligation, but curiosity.
4. Join a group, workshop, or women's circle that stretches your growth.
5. Read books that mirror where you've been and reveal where you can go.

You are not starting over.

You are starting wiser.

# Word for the Soul

There is a season of healing that doesn't feel like healing at all. It feels like being buried. It is dark, quiet, and lonely.

In this season, you may feel forgotten by God and everyone else. This is the sacred space of the soil. It is the holy darkness where roots are formed before a single green shoot breaks the surface.

The pressure you feel is not meant to crush you; it is the force required to break open the hard shell of the seed you have been carrying.

God has not buried you to forget you; He has planted you to grow you.

You are not stuck—you are in the soil.

Let the roots take hold.

Let the seed split open.

Let something new grow right where it hurts.

Trust the unseen work. The sun is coming.

# A Gentle Call to Action: Seeds I Will Plant

Check the ones that speak to your spirit:

☐ Online or in-person training.

☐ A new language or hobby.

☐ Financial wisdom.

☐ Emotional regulation tools.

☐ Something new I've never tried.

☐ Finishing the degree or program I once started.

You don't have to bloom overnight.

You just have to say yes to growth.

And trust... that even this pain has purpose.

# Notes & Reflections

# PRACTICE 14
# THE PRACTICE OF GRATITUDE

*"Give thanks in all circumstances; for this is God's will*
*for you in Christ Jesus."*
*— 1 Thessalonians 5:18 (NIV)*

Gratitude is not about pretending everything is okay.

It's about pausing, even in pain, and remembering that not everything is falling apart.

This scripture isn't calling us to be fake. It's calling us to be faithful. To look for the flickers of light, even while sitting in the shadows.

Gratitude doesn't deny the wound; it simply refuses to let the wound be the whole story.

Giving thanks in all circumstances doesn't mean every moment is good. It means that even in hard moments, God is still good.

Gratitude is the sacred thread that keeps you tethered to truth when everything else feels like it's unraveling.

It steadies the heart.

It grounds the nervous system.

It whispers: "There's still something to be grateful for and worth holding onto."

# Story Time

In Chapter 12 of my memoir, I shared how I learned to say "Thank you" even in the hardest seasons. Gratitude didn't erase my pain, but it reminded me that not everything was falling apart. God was still with me.

There was a season when I woke up overwhelmed. And when I say "season," I mean years. Years of discouragement. Years of hopelessness. Years where I felt like I was barely making it, and no one even knew.

So, I made myself a promise:

Before I touched my phone in the morning, I had to say three things I was grateful for. Some mornings, all I had was:

1. I'm alive.
2. My children are okay.
3. I made it through yesterday.

But over time... I started to notice more.

The way the sunlight touched the curtain.

The peace in the room before anyone else woke up. The part of me that still believed, even if it was just a flicker. Gratitude became an anchor.

It didn't erase my struggle, but it gave me something to stand on inside the struggle. It helped me remember that I was more than what I was going through.

Gratitude slowly trained my eyes: not to ignore the pain, but to notice the provisions. A warm mug in my hands. A text returned. Breath in my lungs. Gratitude didn't fix my life; it fortified my heart so I could live it.

And it reminded me: God was still with me... even here.

# Reflection Prompt

Gently pause and consider:

1. What is one thing (big or small) I am grateful for today?

________________________________________

________________________________________

2. Who am I grateful for and have I told them?

________________________________________

________________________________________

3. How has gratitude softened my heart or lifted my spirit lately?

________________________________________

________________________________________

*Let this moment become sacred. Gratitude is your soul remembering what's still good.*

# Try This

---

*Simple Daily Gratitude*

You don't need hours or a perfect journal, just intention. Try one or more of these:

1. Begin or end your day with 3 things you're thankful for.
2. Keep a small gratitude journal beside your bed.
3. Say your gratitude out loud, let your voice hear it.
4. Thank God for sustaining you, not just for blessing you.
5. Text or call someone just to say: "I'm grateful for you."

Gratitude isn't performance. It is presence.

# Word for the Soul

Gratitude is not about ignoring your pain. It's about anchoring your soul in truth:

That even here... there is still beauty.

Even here... God is still present.

Even here... you are still becoming.

Practicing gratitude:

> Reassures your nervous system that not everything is a threat
> Reconnects you to what is true, not just what is hard
> Shifts your perspective from "What's missing?" to "What's here?"
> Gently reminds you: You've come so far and you're still moving

So, pause. Breathe. Give thanks.

Let your gratitude become your grounding. Let it be the sacred pause between what hurts and what heals. Because even in the valley...

God is still giving you something to say thank You for.

# Notes & Reflections

# PRACTICE 15
# THE PRACTICE OF PRESENCE

*"Be still, and know that I am God:"*
*— Psalm 46:10(a) (KJV)*

To be still is more than a physical pause, it is a soul posture.

It's an invitation to stop striving, stop spiraling, stop escaping, and come home to the now.

Being still doesn't mean pretending everything is okay. It means letting the moment be what it is, without rushing ahead or reaching back.

"Be still, and know..."

> Not guessing.
> Not assuming.
> Not controlling.

But *know*, deep in your spirit, that God is here, even in the stillness.

To be present is to say:

"At this moment, I may not like where I am, but I choose to meet God here. Because I know I am never alone. God is always with me, guiding me, helping me, and showing me the way."

Presence is the sacred practice of meeting peace exactly where you are.

# Story Time

In Chapter 2 of my memoir, I describe how I spent years running from my pain—always in survival mode. But healing taught me to be present, to meet God right where I was, even in the mess.

For so many years, I lived ahead of myself. Always thinking about the next bill... the next crisis... the next heartbreak. My mind would race, and my body would follow.

Even when I sat down, I wasn't still.

My body rested, but my soul kept running. Even when I was with my children, I wasn't truly with them. I was caught in survival. Stuck in the "what-ifs," consumed by the past, and anxious about the future.

I didn't know how to rest. I couldn't hear myself think. I couldn't feel God's nearness... because I wasn't present.

Then one day, in a swirl of overwhelm, I stood still and asked myself: "What's real right now?" And that question changed everything. "What is real right now?"

> My breath.
> My awareness.
> My access to God.
> My choice to pause.

That question became another anchor. Because that moment, even in its imperfection, was enough. Not perfect. But real.

And real was more healing than chasing what I couldn't control.

# Reflection Prompt

Slow down and reflect:

1. What does my body feel like when I'm not present?

______________________________________________

______________________________________________

2. What thoughts or patterns most often pull me away from this moment?

______________________________________________

______________________________________________

3. What helps me return to my breath, my body, my awareness?

______________________________________________

______________________________________________

*Let this moment become sacred. Not because it's perfect, but because it's yours.*

# Try This

---

*Gentle Practices for Presence*

Choose one practice today to anchor yourself in the now:

1.  Take 3 slow, conscious breaths; inhale... pause... exhale... pause.
2.  Say aloud: "Right now, I am safe."
3.  Touch a nearby object. Describe its texture, weight, or temperature.
4.  Name what you feel without judging it: "I feel tired. I feel calm. I feel unsure."
5.  Sit outside for five minutes without your phone.
    Just be.

Presence isn't performance. It is permission.

# Word for the Soul

Being present is not about getting it all right. It's about gently returning to yourself, again, and again. God isn't only in the mountaintop moments. God is in the ordinary.

In your breath.
In your pause.
In your now.

You don't have to relive the past or figure out the future. You don't have to fix, plan, or solve anything at this moment. You just have to be. Right here. Right now.

And that is more than enough.

# Notes & Reflections

# PRACTICE 16
# THE PRACTICE OF REST

*"Rest in the Lord, and wait patiently for Him."*
*— Psalm 37:7 (KJV)*

Rest is not weakness, it is worship.

This verse reminds us that rest is both physical and spiritual. It's not merely about sleep, though our bodies often cry for it. It's about trusting God enough to release what you cannot control.

Sometimes we confuse busyness with holiness. We measure our worth by how much we do, how much we carry, or how much we endure. But God invites us to rest, not because the storm has passed, but because He is present in it.

Rest is not pretending life is easy; it's laying your cares down in the arms of the One who promised to carry them with you.

When you rest in the Lord:

> You tell your body: *It's okay to stop striving.*
> You tell your mind: *You don't have to figure it all out right now.*
> You tell your soul: *God is big enough to hold what feels too heavy for me.*

Rest becomes the sacred rhythm that restores your strength, renews your spirit, and reminds you, *you are already enough.*

# Story Time

In Chapter 12 of my memoir, I describe myself as a living testimony and not a victim.

I remember when my oldest son was robbed at gunpoint, and my car was stolen. I am grateful to God Almighty my son lived to tell what happened.

We lived in a neighborhood where this "wasn't supposed" to happen. Yet it did. This was during the COVID pandemic, when businesses were struggling and people were facing desperation.

I recall the insurance adjuster telling me it might be several weeks before a rental car would be available due to shortages. I told him gently, "I am not going to worry about it. It's all going to work together." And then, instead of spiraling into panic, I whispered a prayer... and I went to sleep.

When I woke up the next morning, I had clarity. I called a friend for a ride, went straight to the rental car company with my COVID mask on, and said: "My car was stolen. I have insurance. I need a rental." And they handed me the keys to an SUV that same day.

It wasn't magic, as if I prayed, slept, woke up, and an hour later drove away in a new car.

At the rental company, I still had to sit and wait for several hours. Yet even there, sitting in a chair, I rested.

Not in panic. Not in despair. Not in fear. I rested my body. I rested my mind. And most of all, I rested in God.

And when they finally handed me the keys, it wasn't just a car I received, it was the reminder that rest resets me for the journey ahead.

There is something sacred about resting in God. It is trust in action. It is the quiet assurance and declaration: My faith is for me to get through.

And I rest in that assurance today.

# Reflection Prompt

Take a moment to reflect:

1. Where have I been resisting rest, convincing myself I have to keep going?

2. What worries keep me awake at night that I can release into God's care?

3. How does my body signal when it needs sacred rest? Do I listen?

*Let this moment become sacred. Rest your mind, body, and soul.*

# Try This

---

*Sacred Rest*

Rest doesn't always mean eight hours of sleep. It can be woven into your day as a practice of worship. Try one:

1. **Sacred Nap**: Give yourself permission to close your eyes for 20 minutes without guilt. Whisper a scripture or prayer before resting.
2. **Blanket + Breath**: Lay down with a soft blanket. Breathe slowly, repeating: "I rest in You, Lord."
3. **Release List**: Before bed, write down the worries you can't control. Place the list in a box or under your Bible as a sign that God is holding them.
4. **Stillness in Waiting**: Next time you're in a waiting room, car line, or checkout line; instead of scrolling your phone, sit back, breathe, and rest in God's presence.

Rest is permission. Rest is prayer. Rest is worship.

# Word for the Soul

Sacred rest is not an escape; it is an embrace. It is the pause that says, God is still God, even while I am still.

When you rest, you release control.
When you rest, you declare trust.
When you rest, you worship.

Caretaker, survivor, parent, leader, friend, you cannot heal without rest.

When your body yawns for its blanket and bed, answer it. When your soul is weary from striving, release it. When your spirit feels restless, let God be your refuge.

Rest in the Lord. Wait patiently for Him. And trust that even in stillness, He is working all things together for your good.

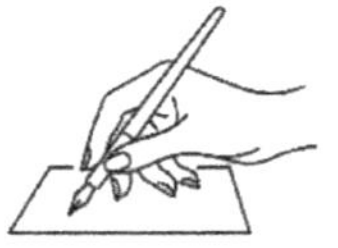

# Notes & Reflections

# FINAL WORD
# A Benediction for Your Journey

*"I have learned, in whatsoever state I am, therewith to be content."*
**– Philippians 4:11 (KJV)**

When I moved to Texas with my children, I did not have a support system. There were days I felt deeply insecure. I worried constantly: What if this happens? What if that happens? What will I do? I would wake up in the middle of the night, overwhelmed by the constant "How will I...?" The fear was real. The thoughts were heavy.

But one morning, I woke up with a song in my heart: "Glory, glory, hallelujah, since I laid my burdens down..." I started singing it, softly at first. Then stronger.

"Burdens down, Lord... burdens down, Lord..."

I sang it over and over, until it became a kind of chant.

And slowly, I could feel something shift. The weight of fear began to lift.

That evening after work, I turned on soft music. I cooked dinner while singing and dancing. I helped my children with their homework. We ate dinner and cleaned up the kitchen. I read to them. I got them ready for bed. And then... I soaked in the tub in silence.

Before I went to sleep, I:

- Wrote down 3 things I was grateful for.
- Prayed for guidance.
- Reflected on ways I could give and create.

That day was not perfect. But it was peaceful.

And that peace became my foundation.

It got me through that day... and many days, weeks, months, and years to come.

# A Prayer for You Because...

Even in these sacred practices, you will not always feel like you are on top of the world.

Some days will feel like valleys. Some moments will be heavy.

But these are the very moments when you can reach for what you now carry:

> A rhythm.
> A prayer.
> A reminder that you are not powerless.
> And with God you are never alone.

These sacred practices are not meant to "fix" you. They are here to ground you, to balance you, and to hold you steady while storms pass.

May this prayer hold space for what you may be still carrying and remind you of what has already been made new.

I Am Not Stuck

Father God, The Breath of Life,

I come before You with open hands and a willing heart.

Not perfect. Not put together. Just present.

Thank You for the strength I didn't know I had.

Thank You for the wisdom I didn't know I needed.

Thank You for the sacred pause in the middle of my pain.

Teach me how to come home to myself.

How to breathe in this moment.

How to trust what I feel and still lean on what is true.

When the world pulls me into the past,

When fear pushes me toward the future,

Anchor me here, in the now.

In Your presence.

In my body.

In this holy ground beneath my feet.

Remind me that healing does not have to look loud.

That joy does not have to be perfect to be real.

That I am not behind.

I am becoming what You have created.

I am not stuck.

I am being shaped.

And even in this valley...

I can still be held.

I can still be loved.

I can still begin again.

Amen.

You made it here through the pages, the sacred practices, and pauses. You showed up for your healing, and that is no small thing. Healing does not mean the pain never happened; it means it no longer holds the same power.

Every breath, prayer, walk, tear, and truth you have embraced has rewired something within you.

You have taught your nervous system that safety is possible, your heart that love is safe again, and your spirit that hope is still alive.

You may not see the fullness of your transformation yet, but heaven does.

God has witnessed every moment you chose to stay, every time you reached for peace instead of panic, grace instead of guilt, faith instead of fear.

Keep practicing what brings you home to yourself.

These sacred practices of breathing, bathing, singing, creating, praying, and resting. I still use them. Some weekly. Most daily. They ground me. They remind me. They empower me to listen to my body and move from a place of embodied faith.

You do not have to escape where you are. You don't have to force a breakthrough. You do not have to wait to be rescued. You can start right here.

- With your breath.
- With your voice.
- With your body.
- With your presence.
- With small, sacred practices that remind you:

You are not stuck—you are being shaped.

You are not broken—you are being built.

***Return to these sacred practices whenever life feels heavy or unfamiliar.***

Remember, healing is not a destination; it is a rhythm of remembering who you are and whose you are.

You are the healer and the healed. The teacher and the testimony.

What you have walked through will become light for someone else's path.

So, take a deep breath.

Place your hand on your heart. Whisper this truth to your soul.

With love and solidarity,

Amanda

# Notes & Reflections

# Resources for Your Healing Journey

## Disclaimer:

These resources are provided for educational and informational purposes only and are not a substitute for professional care, diagnosis, or treatment.

If you are in danger or in crisis, call **911** immediately.

If you or someone you know is experiencing thoughts of self-harm or suicide, call or text **988** (the Suicide and Crisis Lifeline) for immediate, confidential support, available **24/7**.

## National and Crisis Support Helplines:

- **988 Suicide and Crisis Lifeline**

  Call or text **988** or visit 988lifeline.org for free, confidential support 24 hours a day.

- **Crisis Text Line**

  Text **HOME** to **741741** to connect with a trained crisis counselor anytime. Visit crisistextline.org for additional support options.

- **National Domestic Violence Hotline**

  Call **1-800-799-7233 (SAFE)** or text **START** to **88788**.
  Visit thehotline.org for live chat, safety planning,
  and survivor resources 24 hours a day.

- **National Sexual Assault Hotline (RAINN)**

  Call **1-800-656-HOPE (4673)** or visit rainn.org for
  confidential support and referrals to
  local service providers 24 hours a day.

---

# Mental Health & Therapy:

- **National Alliance on Mental Illness (NAMI)**

  Call the NAMI HelpLine at **1-800-950-6264**
  or text **HELPLINE** to **62640** for information and support.
  Website: nami.org

- **Psychology Today – Find a Therapist**

  Search for licensed therapists, counselors, or social workers in your area.
  Website: psychologytoday.com/us/therapists

- **Therapy for Black Girls / Therapy for Black Men**

  Culturally competent therapist directories and community content.
  Website: therapyforblackgirls.com and therapyforblackmen.org

---

# Veterans and First Responders:

- **Veterans Crisis Line**

  Call **988** then **press 1**, or text **838255**, or
  chat online at veteranscrisisline.net
  Confidential support for veterans and their loved ones.

- **Safe Call Now**

  Crisis referral service for public safety employees,
  first responders, and their families.
  Call **1-206-459-3020** or visit safecallnow.org

# Addiction and Recovery:

- **SAMHSA National Helpline**

  Call **1-800-662-HELP (4357)** for free,
  confidential treatment referral and
  information on substance use or mental health services.
  Website: samhsa.gov/find-help/national-helpline

- **Celebrate Recovery**

  Christ-centered recovery groups for those
  overcoming hurts, habits, or hang-ups.
  Website: celebraterecovery.com

# Children, Teens, and Families:

- **Childhelp National Child Abuse Hotline**

  Call or text **1-800-422-4453** or
  chat online at childhelphotline.org

- **National Runaway Safeline**

  For youth in crisis or those thinking about running away.
  Call **1-800-RUNAWAY (786-2929)** or
  visit 1800runaway.org.

# Books That Helped Me Heal:

- Triggered to Heal: An Invitation to Feel Fully and Heal Deeply – Amanda Ligon, LMSW (my personal story of trauma recovery and resilience)
- The Body Keeps the Score – Bessel van der Kolk, M.D.
- What Happened to You? – Dr. Bruce D. Perry and Oprah Winfrey
- The Greatest Salesman in the World – Og Mandino
- The Alchemist – Paulo Coelho
- The Purpose Driven Life – Rick Warren

# Spiritual Tools & Grounding Practices:

- You Version Bible App – www.bible.com
  Daily scripture, devotionals, and guided prayer plans.
- Insight Timer App – www.insighttimer.com
  Free meditations, music, and breathwork tools.
- Abide App – www.abide.com
  Christian meditation and sleep stories rooted in scripture.
- The Healing Table – letsconnect@mannasmission.org
  Healing tools, community support, and personal coaching led by Amanda.

# Create Your Own Healing Space:

These are items that supported my daily grounding:

- Journal + favorite pen
- Soft instrumental or worship music
- Scented candle or essential oil diffuser
- Epsom salt + herbs for intentional baths
- A cozy chair or floor cushion for quiet reflection
- A playlist that makes your soul feel safe

# REFERENCES

Harris, J. I., Erbes, C. R., Engdahl, B. E., Thuras, P., Ogden, H., Olson, R. H. A., Winskowski, A. M., Bacon, R., Malec, C., Campion, K., & Le, T. (2011). The effectiveness of a trauma-focused spiritually integrated intervention for veterans exposed to trauma. Journal of Clinical Psychology, 67(5), 425–438. https://doi.org/10.1002/jclp.20777.

Park, C. L., Smith, P. H., Lee, S. Y., Mazure, C. M., McKee, S. A., & Hoff, R. (2017). Positive and negative religious/spiritual coping and combat exposure as predictors of posttraumatic stress and perceived growth in Iraq and Afghanistan veterans. Psychology of Religion and Spirituality, 9(1), 13–20 https://doi.org/10.1037/rel0000086.

U.S. Department of Veterans Affairs, National Center for PTSD. (n.d.). Spirituality and resilience. Retrieved October 25, 2025, from https://www.ptsd.va.gov/professional/treat/care/toolkits/clergy/spiritualityResilience.asp.

Larsen, S. E. (n.d.). Addressing religious or spiritual dimensions of trauma and PTSD. U.S. Department of Veterans Affairs, National Center for PTSD. Retrieved October 25, 2025, from https://www.ptsd.va.gov/professional/treat/txessentials/spirituality_trauma.asp.

# ACKNOWLEDGEMENTS

This book was born during early quiet mornings, as I sat with my breath and listened to my heartbeat. In that stillness, I was not writing, I was remembering. I was returning to myself.

To every survivor of sexual assault and domestic violence: I acknowledge your courage, your silence, your voice, and your becoming. This book carries pieces of your story too. May it meet you with gentleness.

To the advocates and healers that I work with in this sacred work: Thank you for showing up, for bearing witness, for holding space, and for reminding others that healing is possible.

To my children, thank you for walking closely beside me as I walked this out. Your love, presence, and patience gave me the strength to keep breathing, to keep believing, and to keep moving.

To my two Buds, my godmother, each one of my amazing friends, and my spiritual teachers & partners, I LOVE YOU and I am Grateful for YOU!!

# ABOUT THE AUTHOR

Amanda D. Ligon, LMSW, is a Licensed Social Worker, Trauma Support Partner, Decluttering Coach, Minister, and the visionary founder of No Violence No Victim Inc., a nonprofit advocating for survivors of domestic violence; The Healing Table, her life coaching practice where she guides women from survival to sacred restoration; and Manna's Mission STHC, which provides housing referrals and compassionate support for individuals experiencing homelessness, with a special focus on older people.

Born from a raped pregnancy and into homelessness, Amanda is a survivor of childhood sexual abuse, sex trafficking, rape, poverty, and over two decades of intimate partner violence within a marriage. Yet her story is not one of victimhood, it is one of divine survival, soul reclamation, and purpose.

Faith has been the foundation of Amanda's healing journey. In her darkest moments, when no one came to rescue her, she learned to anchor herself in the truth that God saw her, knew her name, and was walking with her through every valley. Scripture became her anchor. Prayer became her lifeline. And the belief that she was never alone gave her the strength to rescue herself and break generational cycles of abuse.

Amanda's work is deeply rooted in both clinical expertise and spiritual truth. As a Licensed Social Worker, she brings evidence-based, trauma-informed care to her clients. As a Minister, she brings the healing power of faith, Scripture, and the assurance that God is present in every step of the healing journey. She believes that faith and professional support work together, not against each other and that true healing addresses the whole person: mind, body, spirit, and relationships.

She is a proud mother of four (two sons and two daughters), a bonus daughter, a beloved grandmother, sister, and aunt. Amanda has mentored youth in public schools for over a decade, using her voice and testimony to inspire courage and healing. She has worked with older people for over 25 years in hospitals, residential homes, nursing facilities, and on the streets—always meeting people where they are—with dignity.

Since 2002, she has devoted herself to housing families below the poverty line. As a Licensed Social Worker and Advocate, Amanda walks closely with survivors of domestic violence and sexual abuse, offering trauma-informed care and holistic support.

Amanda also creates handmade wellness tools including herbal bath soaks, facial steams, and natural hair oils through her healing practice Manna's Nature.

Her debut memoir, *Triggered to Heal: An Invitation to Feel Fully and Heal Deeply*, is a powerful blend of personal testimony, embodied wisdom, and spiritual truth. Through her words and her work, Amanda offers a sacred invitation to break habitual cycles, reclaim your voice, and remember that healing is possible, you are never alone, and you are always being guided by a God who sees you and loves you.